THE STATES AND THEIR SYMBOLS

Wyoming
Facts and Symbols

by Muriel L. Dubois

Consultant:
Heyward Schrock
Curator of Education
Wyoming State Museum

Capstone
press
Mankato, Minnesota

Capstone Press
151 Good Counsel Drive, P.O. Box 669, Mankato, Minnesota 56002
http://www.capstone-press.com

Library of Congress Cataloging-in-Publication Data
Dubois, Muriel L.
　Wyoming facts and symbols/by Muriel L Dubois.—Rev. and updated ed.
　p. cm.—(The states and their symbols)
　Includes bibliographical references (p. 23) and index.
　Summary: Presents information about the state of Wyoming, its nickname, motto, and emblems.
　ISBN 0-7368-2281-X (hardcover)
　1. Emblems, State—Wyoming—Juvenile literature. [1. Emblems, State—Wyoming. 2. Wyoming.] I. Title. II. Series.
CR203.W8 D83　2003
978.7—dc21　　　　　　　　　　　　　　　　　　　　　2002154905

Editorial Credits
Christianne C. Jones, update editor; Tom Adamson, editor; Linda Clavel, production designer and illustrator; Alta Schaffer, update photo researcher; Kimberly Danger, photo researcher

Photo Credits
John Elk III, 10, 22 (all)
One Mile Up, Inc., 8, 10 (insert)
Robert McCaw, 18
Root Resources/Alan G. Nelson, 12; Anthony Mercieca, 20
Unicorn Stock Photos/Rod Furgason, 6; Tommy Dodson, 14; Alice M. Prescott, 16
Visuals Unlimited/Joe McDonald, cover

1 2 3 4 5 6 08 07 06 05 04 03

Table of Contents

Map 4
Fast Facts 5
State Name and Nickname 7
State Seal and Motto 9
State Capitol and Flag 11
State Bird 13
State Tree 15
State Flower 17
State Mammal 19
More State Symbols 21

Places to Visit 22
Words to Know 23
Read More 23
Useful Addresses 24
Internet Sites 24
Index 24

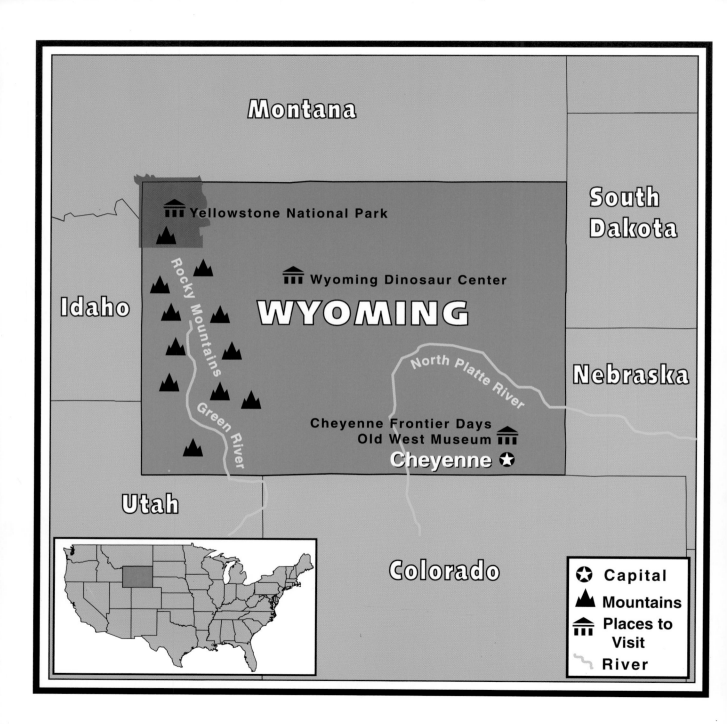

Fast Facts

Capital: Cheyenne is the capital of Wyoming.

Largest City: Cheyenne is the largest city in Wyoming. More than 53,000 people live there.

Size: Wyoming is the tenth largest state. It covers 97,818 square miles (253,349 square kilometers).

Location: Wyoming is in the western United States.

Population: 493,782 people live in Wyoming (2000 U.S. Census Bureau).

Statehood: On July 10, 1890, Wyoming became the 44th state to join the United States.

Natural Resources: Wyoming has coal, crude oil, and gas. Workers mine bentonite to make water softeners, toothpaste, and makeup.

Manufactured Goods: Wyoming workers produce chemical and mineral products, wood products, and machinery.

Crops: Wyoming farmers raise sheep for wool and cattle for beef. They grow sugar beets, barley, beans, corn, and hay.

State Name and Nickname

Wyoming's name comes from a Native American language. The words "mecheweami-ing" mean "at the big plains" or "on the great plain." Early settlers used the name Wyoming because it was similar to the Native American words. They thought the words described the area well.

Wyoming's official nickname is the Equality State. In 1869, the territorial government of Wyoming gave women the right to vote. It was the first government in the United States to do this.

Wyoming sometimes is called the Cowboy State. Rodeos are held all over the state. A rodeo is a cowboy competition. Men, women, and children compete. They show their skills in roping cattle and riding horses.

Rodeos are popular events in Wyoming.

Wyoming's government adopted its state seal in 1893. The seal represents Wyoming's government. It also makes state government papers official.

A statue of a woman stands in the center of the seal. She holds a banner that says "Equal Rights." Pillars are on each side of the statue. Scrolls wind around the pillars. The words on the scrolls are livestock, mines, oil, and grain. These businesses are important to Wyoming's economy.

The shield below the statue's feet has the number "44" on it. In 1890, Wyoming became the 44th state to join the United States. The eagle above the number stands for the United States.

Wyoming's motto is "Equal Rights." Wyoming has supported voting rights for women for more than 130 years. In 1924, Nellie Tayloe Ross became the governor of Wyoming. She was the first female governor in the United States.

The man on the right stands for mining. The man on the left represents the livestock business.

State Capitol and Flag

Cheyenne is the capital of Wyoming. Wyoming's capitol building is in Cheyenne. Government officials meet there to make Wyoming's laws.

Workers completed Wyoming's capitol in 1888. The building is made of gray sandstone granite. Wyoming's capitol looks like the U.S. Capitol in Washington, D.C.

Government officials adopted the Wyoming state flag on January 31, 1917. The flag uses the same colors as the U.S. flag. The outside border of the Wyoming flag is red and white. Red represents Wyoming's Native Americans and the blood of the pioneers. White represents the goodness in Wyoming's citizens.

The blue rectangle on the flag stands for Wyoming's sky and mountains. Blue also is the color of justice. A bison, or American buffalo, is in the center of the rectangle. The state seal is in the center of the bison.

Some of the stones used to build the capitol came from Colorado. The rest came from Rawlins, Wyoming.

State Bird

Wyoming's state bird is the western meadowlark. The meadowlark is a songbird. Louis Freudenthal of Thermopolis, Wyoming, suggested the meadowlark be named the state bird. He wrote about it in a school essay. The state university and some state clubs agreed with him. Wyoming adopted the meadowlark as the state bird in 1927.

The meadowlark is about 9 inches (23 centimeters) long. The bird has a yellow breast with a black "V" at its neck. Streaks of brown, white, and gray are on its head and back. The meadowlark's colors help it hide in tall prairie grasses. Hawks who hunt the meadowlark cannot see the birds there.

The meadowlark builds its nest in grass. The nest is shaped like a cup. Female meadowlarks lay about five eggs at one time. The eggs are white with brown and purple spots.

The black "V" on the western meadowlark's neck is its most noticeable feature.

State Tree

Wyoming adopted the plains cottonwood as its state tree in 1947. Pioneers planted the plains cottonwood because it grew well in Wyoming's changing weather.

The plains cottonwood can grow 50 to 60 feet (15 to 18 meters) tall. The tree grows quickly but does not live as long as some other types of trees.

People plant the cottonwood for many reasons. Cottonwoods can help stop erosion. The tree's roots hold soil in place. The roots keep soil from being worn away by water and wind. People also use cottonwood lumber to make buildings, furniture, and paper.

In 1990, a plains cottonwood in Albany County, Wyoming, was named the largest cottonwood in the world. At the time, it was more than 64 feet (19.5 meters) tall. The tree's trunk was 31 feet (9.5 meters) around.

The cottonwood's leaves change color in the fall.

State Flower

The Indian paintbrush is a prairie flower. It became Wyoming's state flower in 1917. Indian paintbrushes grow nearly everywhere in the state.

The tips of the Indian paintbrush look like they have been dipped in paint. The tips can be red, orange, purple, or yellow. These colorful parts of the plant are called bracts.

A bract is a small, showy leaf on a flower stalk. On many plants, bracts are small and hidden. Indian paintbrush bracts are large and colorful. These colorful parts of the plant are not the flower. The actual flower is a small green blossom. The Indian paintbrush can grow from 6 inches to 3 feet (15 to 91 centimeters) tall.

The bracts on the Indian paintbrush look like flower petals.

State Mammal

In 1985, Wyoming adopted the bison as its state mammal. The bison is the largest land mammal in North America. A male bison can grow up to 6 feet (1.8 meters) tall. It can weigh 2,000 pounds (900 kilograms). Young bison are red-brown. They become darker as they get older.

Until the 1830s, millions of bison roamed the western plains. Native Americans hunted bison for hundreds of years. They ate bison meat and used the hide for clothing and shelter. They made rope and thread from the bison's tendons. They did not waste any part of the animal.

When settlers moved west, they killed bison for sport and food. The bison nearly became extinct.

The bison no longer is in danger of becoming extinct. People have worked hard to save the bison. More than 3,000 bison now roam parts of Wyoming, including Yellowstone National Park.

The bison also is called the American buffalo.

State Dinosaur: In 1994, officials chose the Triceratops as Wyoming's state dinosaur. Scientists have found Triceratops fossils in Wyoming.

State Fish: State officials named the cutthroat trout as Wyoming's state fish in 1987. Fishers in Wyoming like to catch cutthroat trout.

State Fossil: People found knightia fossils in southwestern Wyoming. The knightia was a kind of fish. It could grow up to 6 inches (15 centimeters) long. The knightia became the state fossil in 1987.

State Gemstone: In 1967, jade became Wyoming's state gemstone. Wyoming jade can be green or black. People use jade to make jewelry and statues.

State Reptile: In 1993, Wyoming adopted the horned toad as the state reptile. Horned toads are lizards. Their bodies are flat and wide. They have spiky skin that looks like a toad's skin. A horned toad raises its body off the hot sand to stay cool.

Horned toads usually are the color of their surroundings. This coloring allows them to hide from predators.

Places to Visit

Cheyenne Frontier Days Old West Museum

Cheyenne Frontier Days is a yearly celebration of the Old West. It takes place in Cheyenne. This event features rodeos, country music concerts, and western art shows. The Old West Museum also is in Cheyenne. Visitors see horse-drawn carriages and Native American costumes.

Wyoming Dinosaur Center and Dig Sites

The Wyoming Dinosaur Center in Thermopolis has one of the largest fossil quarries in the world. Visitors age eight and older help staff members dig for fossils during Dig for a Day. The center's museum contains full-sized fossil skeletons of 14 dinosaurs, including Triceratops.

Yellowstone National Park

Yellowstone National Park was the country's first national park. Visitors camp, hike, ride horses, or ride on a stagecoach. Elk, bison, bighorn sheep, and many other wild animals live in the park. Yellowstone has 200 to 250 active geysers. The most famous geyser is called Old Faithful.

Words to Know

bentonite (BEN-tin-ite)—a type of clay formed from volcanic ash; workers in Wyoming mine bentonite.

extinct (ek-STINGKT)—no longer living anywhere in the world

fossil (FOSS-uhl)—plant or animal remains preserved in rock

geyser (GYE-zur)—an underground spring that shoots hot water and steam through a hole in the ground

mammal (MAM-uhl)—a warm-blooded animal with a backbone

plain (PLANE)—a large, flat area of treeless land

scroll (SKROHL)—a roll of paper with writing on it

tendon (TEN-duhn)—a strong band of tissue that joins a muscle to a bone

territory (TER-uh-tor-ee)—land that belongs to a country

Read More

Kent, Deborah. *Wyoming.* Hello U.S.A. New York: Children's Press, 2002.

Kummer, Patricia K. *Wyoming.* One Nation. Mankato, Minn.: Capstone Press, 2003.

Parker, Janice. *Wyoming.* A Kid's Guide to American States. Mankato, Minn.: Weigl Publishers, 2001.

Useful Addresses

Secretary of State
State Capitol Building
Cheyenne, WY 82002

**Wyoming Tourism and State
Marketing Division**
I-25 at College Drive
Cheyenne, WY 82002

Internet Sites

Do you want to find out more about Wyoming?
Let FactHound, our fact-finding hound dog, do the
research for you.

Here's how:
1) Visit **http://www.facthound.com**
2) Type in the **BOOK ID** number:
   073682281X
3) Click on **FETCH IT**.

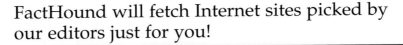

FactHound will fetch Internet sites picked by
our editors just for you!

Index

bison, 11, 19
bract, 17
cutthroat trout, 21
Equality State, 7
government, 7, 9, 11
horned toad, 21
Indian paintbrush, 17

jade, 21
knightia fossils, 21
plains cottonwood, 15
rodeo, 7
Ross, Nellie Tayloe, 9
Triceratops, 21
western meadowlark, 13